Things to Know Before You Go

Shana McLean Moore

DEDICATION

With gratitude...

To the **one** who is my rock, the love of my life, the funniest guy this side of the 101: Russ

To the **two** who make my heart burst with purpose and pride, and teach me to pay attention to how things ought to be: Tori and Taylor

To the **two** who have given me the ultimate gift of unconditional love since day one: Marcia and Bill

To the **one** who gives me thick skin and so many reasons to donkey laugh: Matt (and his **three** lovelies: Meredith, Courtney, and Kasey)

To the **six** who came to me as the sweetest package deal when I met Russ: Harry and Sue, Jeff and Mindy, Rick and Gyen

To the **31** who validate the journey we share as women and mothers, who are by my side to celebrate, mourn, connect, and grow. Whether we met as children, teachers, blacktop moms, or writers, I cherish your friendship.

CONTENTS

ACKNOWLEDGMENTS

Thank you to my three favorite feelers and thinkers, Glennon Doyle, Brené Brown, and Oprah Winfrey. Following your work and seeing the response of your readers reminds me that there are good and thoughtful people all around us who are eager to improve our communities and our world. I am so grateful for your collective inspiration to step into the arena and live my best "brutiful" life.

INTRODUCTION

This book started off as a gift/one final nag to my children before they went off to college.

As our firstborn's dorm move-in day inched closer and closer, I kept thinking about all the things a person needs to know before launching into the world on their own and found myself with one panicked thought after another:

"Wait! Have I taught her THAT?"

Soon, my growing list that had started out as a tactical itemizing of how-to's began to sound as clinical and exhaustive as an operating manual for the mini fridge we had just ordered her.

Then it dawned on me (probably after reading an article about helicopter moms) that all the immunization forms, roommate agreements, food plan choices, and insurance forms are perfectly manageable (though admittedly still soul-sucking) when a person has the right mindset for living and learning and connecting with people.

So, sometime over these past five years of sending my kids out and welcoming them back, I cooled my copter blades and decided that it might be more effective and enjoyable for all if I concentrated, instead, on channeling my motherly wisdom toward how to prepare a heart and spirit for all the "adulting" the world expects of us.

And, alas, I do mean *us*.

As I focused on writing this grown-up guide of the A to Z of attitudes and qualities that position a person for an engaging, purposeful, and successful life, I began to realize that I was writing it as much for my own needs as I was for my children.

With the departure of one child and then the other, I found myself embarking on a new chapter of adulthood for myself, one that was currently lacking in the same levels of purpose and engagement than the one that preceded it.

On the days when I felt lonely, defeated, or uninspired, I looked to the thinkers and writers who gave (and continue to give) me hope to take on the work, the people, and, eventually, the time to connect and create.

I do not read them as research—I read them because the quest to live a positive and rewarding life is fragile and, if I am not deliberate, the life events that enter into my to-do list for the day can derail me. Whether I will let them or not is my daily decision to make.

And I need the reminder as often as I hope to pass it along to others.

While I acknowledge that many of life's lessons require the touching of the proverbial wet paint so you can be sure as shit that there is a valid reason for the "Do Not Touch" sign, I sleep a bit better at night knowing that I have spelled out where I stand on some subjects that matter.

Will there still be bumps in the road if you take my advice? You bet. Even some craters that will deflate you upon impact.

Be patient with yourself. You have to make mistakes to learn life's lessons on your own. I'm just hoping that my whispers echo through your mind when you experience these moments for yourself so that you'll learn your lessons the first time they feel real to you.

If you learn them early enough, you will find yourself living your life with a whole and hardy heart that makes you feel alive and hopeful for your present and your future.

Whether you are someone's daughter or son, mother or father, my wish, from A to Z, is that each of these *Things to Know Before You Go* refuels your spirit before you step back out the door and face your corner of the world.

A IS FOR AWESOME PEOPLE

✓*infectiously positive attitude*

✓*inspiring work ethic*

✓*quirky sense of creativity*

✓*ability to connect with people and draw the best out of them*

✓*resilient spirit that allows them to suffer big setbacks but never give up*

✓*definitely not an asshole*

Have you ever stopped to think about what makes the awesome people in your life stand out?

While the people we typically consider to be awesome are the very picture of success, the cool thing to discover – when contemplating those we admire – is that this success has many definitions.

Sure, it may include the traditional association with achievement, but more often than not this awesomeness can be attributed to qualities of their heart and spirit and not just their minds and bank accounts.

When you reflect on the people you know who fit this description, I hope you will be brave and answer this question honestly:

Do the awesome people in your life inspire or intimidate you?

In other words, do you want to spend time with them because they challenge you to raise your game, or do you keep your distance because you feel like you pale in comparison?

How you answer this question says a lot about who you are and where you're going. The good news is that it's never too late to change your mindset.

In fact, your own success may depend on it.

If you shy away from the movers, the shakers, and the doers around you, what you're doing by default is surrounding yourself with mediocrity... or worse. This matters because the people you spend your days with are what helps you define your sense of what is acceptable for yourself.

If every person around you spends half their day sleeping, high, un-employed, living on a diet of fast food, or having low expectations for what they expect from a job, a friend, or a lover, this becomes your idea of what "everyone" does, because it is all that you see day in and day out.

If, instead, you spend your time surrounded by people who are hitting the gym, taking classes, reading books, working hard to get promoted, and are determined to maintain a level of physical and emotional wellness, *this* type of living becomes your view of normal, your world view, your culture.

Put another way, as motivational speaker Jim Rohn famously said, "we are the average of the five people we spend the most time with."

Think about this in the most personal way. Who are your five people? How are they affecting the composition of YOU as a byproduct of your time spent with them?

When it comes to our relationships, we are greatly impacted by those closest to us. Our time spent with them affects our way of thinking, our self-esteem, and our decisions. Sure, everyone is their own person, but research shows that we're more affected by our environment than we think. It behooves us, then, to be very purposeful about the environment we create for ourselves. We need to walk toward, not away from, people whose light, drive, and zest for living might feel intimidating to us.

Why? Because they are not only exciting to be around, but we also want the rub-off effect of their dynamism to become our expectation for ourselves.

We must squash our impulse to be intimidated or competitive with such people and remind ourselves that scarcity is a real thing for physical resources, but it is a lie when projected onto people. You see, the best part about awesomeness is its infiniteness.

You may be thinking, "Well, there's not much awesome in me, so I guess that leaves even more for the rest of the universe."

The thing is, we all have some of that self-doubt. Even (or especially so) the blustery types like Kanye West who want us to believe they are up to their wazoos in awesome.

Each one of us knows there's always room for improvement within us. We could always be a little better, faster, stronger, smarter, kinder, richer, thinner, more clever, or more admired. So could anyone really think they've reached the pinnacle of success and believe they will hold the title for a lifetime? Of course not.

The only difference between those who feel un-awesome and those who sit confidently in their value is that awesome people don't let their self-doubt paralyze them. They push through the fear and keep making progress toward their goals.

These people are also kind to themselves because they've accepted that being awesome doesn't mean they have to achieve all of their goals. The awesome is in the go-for-it spirit that leaves them trying when so many others give up.

The other thing that awesome people know is that you going after yours isn't any threat to me going after mine. In fact, if we talk to each other about our goals, and encourage one another toward meeting them, we increase the possibility that we'll *both* achieve ours.

So, don't feel threatened by other people's success. Use theirs as inspiration to go after your own. If you surround yourself with enough of these people who are awesome in their own individual ways, awesome will become the norm, the culture of what you and your people do.

THINGS TO KNOW BEFORE YOU GO

B IS FOR BE BRAVE

Imagine, if you will, a friendly game of *Family Feud* where contestants are asked for the top-reported answer to the question, "Who are the bravest people in the land?"

Survey says... first responders.

Really, who else could fill the top spot? Whether they are rushing into a burning building to save lives and structures, catching criminals in the act, or are boots-on-the-ground soldiers fighting for our freedom and safety, these people and the work they do are the definition of bravery because they run toward situations that most of us would run away from.

And while that type of bravery is awe-inspiring, you don't need to be a hero to show bravery in your own life. Sure, there will be no medals for this kind of bravery, but there *will* be an immense amount of personal gratification when you make the bold decision to risk the possibility of rejection, failure, and possibly even physical harm in order to:

- Show up authentically as the person you truly are

- Grow and stretch your abilities by pushing yourself to do hard things

- Stand up for people and causes you believe in

Bravery in authenticity:

"Because true belonging only happens when we present our authentic, imperfect selves to the world, our sense of belonging can never be greater than our level of self-acceptance." — Brené Brown

We've all spent time with someone who doesn't "get" us. It's a terrible, lonely feeling, right? The sense of *ugh* is compounded when we spend time with a whole group of people who seem to think and act alike and enjoy one another's company immensely while we feel like the ones who don't fit in. But here's the thing... those people are entitled to be happy and thriving together in the same way *you* are entitled to be happy and thriving with people who get you. There is someone for everyone in this vast world of ours—we all just need to find our people, the ones who give us the sense of being home in their company.

Before we can feel at home with others, though, we must feel at home with ourselves. We have to come to terms with the fact that even though we are not perfect, we are still worthy and deserving of love.

The interesting thing about this is that once we are at peace within ourselves about our perceived inadequacies, we exude a quiet kind of self-acceptance that leaves others feeling drawn to us. It makes the right people feel attracted to our company so that our circle becomes one of sincere belonging.

But it isn't just a coming to terms with how we come up short, either—it is also being able to truly own our strengths, instead of trying to downplay them to make others feel less intimidated. As the wise Marianne Williamson says, "As we let our own light shine, we unconsciously give other people permission to do the same. As we are liberated from our own fear, our presence automatically liberates others."

Bravery in growth:

Each one of us brave enough to admit it battles some degree of the imposter syndrome, questioning why we – in a world full of other talented, charming, and smart people – might be the best person qualified for the job, the role, or the partnership.

The thing is that the only way to keep growing is to put ourselves out there despite the very real possibility that there are others just as qualified or deserving... or more.

Whether it is inviting a potential new friend to hang out, ask someone on a date, audition for a role in a play, try out for a sports team, sing a solo, sign up for a competitive race, become the founder of a new club or business, fill out a job application, or speak our truth, we are presented with opportunities to grow and stretch our physical and emotional abilities every single day.

When we accept these types of challenges, we are making a declaration about our spirit and our desire to become better, smarter, faster than we were yesterday. And when we manage to succeed at these challenges, the level of personal satisfaction we experience is ten times sweeter than whenever some piece of good fortune just falls into our lap. Why? Because we pushed ourselves and prevailed, and earned the success we achieved.

Will you sometimes suck? And fail? And be so, so, SO disappointed? Yes, you will. But from the failures, you will learn. You will stay humble. You will persevere. You will grow and you will learn to appreciate the wins after experiencing losses.

And please don't even wish for success to fall into your lap. You need the journey just as much as you want the destination. Every single human needs a reason to get out of bed in the morning—whether it is for people who need them, work that calls them, or some other type of pursuit that stimulates their personal growth.

The greater your purpose, the more likely you will be to take on the challenges that require you to face the world with bravery.

Bravery in being an upstander:

"It takes a great deal of bravery to stand up to our enemies, but just as much to stand up to our friends." — J.K. Rowling

Another way to be brave is to be prepared to step forward when someone else, be it a friend or stranger, is in need of some backup. It is a scary and risky thing to do, but it is such a powerful way to show support for people and ideals that you believe in. Whether it is an instance of live bullying or cyber trolling, prepare yourself to take a stand with anyone being victimized so that they will feel less alone and afraid.

This, by the way, is as true for how you treat individuals as it is for how you respond to causes that may not even affect you directly, but that you choose to support because of your sense of what is right and what is wrong.

Be the personal, cape-less hero of someone else's backstory.

And your own.

C IS FOR CHOOSE YOUR ATTITUDE

· Debit or credit? Printed receipt or electronic? Guacamole, even though it's extra?

We make a zillion choices a day. But do you ever stop to think about **how** you choose to respond to all the things that come at you? The truth is that there are always at least two ways you can respond, and your first instinct may need to be clubbed over the head in favor of a more positive, less victimizing second choice.

Case in point #1:

How do you feel when you see friends post pictures of an event you weren't invited to? The easy, instinctive response is to feel slighted and sad, even mad. As difficult as it is, it's best to treat these feelings like you would an impassioned game of Whack-a-Mole.

You want to know why?

You're probably thinking I will say that you should be happy that your friends are out enjoying life. While that is true and evolved and very, very lovely, it may be a level of enlightenment that one can't achieve until quite old and wise, and maybe even until their first name is Mother and their last name rhymes with Manresa.

Instead, I hope you will choose to analyze the situation. Sometimes the answer is chalked up to spontaneity, or the number of open seats in a car. But other times it's actually you. Do you turn down offers often enough that your friends start to think, *why bother?*

Do you ever invite anyone over or organize an outing, or do you just expect everyone to come to you? If you usually make time for them and organize outings and they still don't include you, it might be time to choose to spend time with other people who actually appreciate you.

Or, this part is harder to digest, maybe your behavior comes across as selfish, mean, or annoying and this is your wake-up call to work on having the kind of attitude that draws people in, instead of pushing them away.

I hope you'll choose an empowered response instead of feeling like a victim. Ask yourself: How is my behavior affecting my social life? Do I need to reach out more? Do I need to find new people who appreciate me for who I am? Do I need to work on being a more positive person that people would want to include?

Case in point #2:

Speaking of attitude, do you ever catch yourself saying "this is boring?" If you do, you're declaring the choice you've made. You're actually choosing for this event to suck. I don't typically advocate violence, but I hope you'll use your club to make like a caveman and beat this impulse unconscious.

The truth is that having fun doesn't just happen upon you. Your attitude and actions are what determine if you have a good time or not. You could be at Disneyland and have a rotten time just as easily as you could sit on a ladder with your friend in someone's stinky, windowless garage and have the best time of your life. It all depends on what you choose to bring to the situation: your best self, or your blah self.

Who do you know who tends to bring their best self to your interactions with them? Who walks on the sunny side? What do you think makes them seem so (damn) happy all the time?

As someone who has likely inspired an eye roll or two in her day due to Excessive Use of Cheer (or EUC), I'd like to debunk a couple of myths about happy people.

Myth #1: Happy people are always happy

People who show emotion so visibly and palpably feel things deeply. And, alas, there is no way to intensely feel positive emotions and selectively block out negative ones. This means that people who present themselves as particularly happy, not only as a mood but as an overriding temperament, have developed a filter that allows the good stuff they feel to go out and dance on tables while the tough stuff whispers quietly in a corner booth.

The unspoken M.O. of these happy people is to share their burdens only with their trusted inner circle while shielding the masses from the type of energy that could leave them feeling down. So, when a bad mood strikes, happy people make the choice to contain their toxic spill by sopping up and neutralizing their negative emotions (in constructive ways) so they don't seep out and harm everyone they encounter.

This winds up being a gift both to the people they spend time with and to themselves. Since, many times, the burdens they carry aren't really going away, they choose, instead, to take their mind from broken-record mode and move the needle to a new mental groove.

Myth #2: Happy people are happy because their lives are easier than yours

The easy road to take when confronted with someone who seems to like their life more than you like yours is to tell yourself, "Well, their problems are so miniscule compared to mine."

Here's what age and wisdom have taught me: every single person has things they love about their life, things that make them feel *meh*, and things that outright rot that they'd really like to change.

It really boils down to what we want to focus our energy on: being the person who walks under their own personal cloud, or being the person who radiates the light of hope that makes people feel like we're all going to be okay.

"Darkness cannot drive out darkness; only light can do that. Hate cannot drive out hate; only love can do that."

— *Martin Luther King, Jr.*

Before we can be a source of light to others, we must first invite it into our selves and our environment. I mean this quite literally.

As the gatekeeper to your own spirit, what do you allow in that you could deny entry? We all have dark and difficult situations and people that we have to deal with, but what about the optional things that you could replace with some light and levity?

When it comes to your physical surroundings, do you open the blinds to allow in physical light? Letting in the daylight is a proven trick for lifting your spirits. And I'm equally convinced that allowing fresh air to replace the thick, funky smell of cooped up humans with a little outdoor breeze is as helpful for your lungs as it is your psyche. Heck, throw in the sound of chirping birds and you might even find yourself humming Disney tunes.

Speaking of physical space, do you manage your clutter so that it doesn't feel like it is closing in on you? It is much easier to feel calm and centered when we feel like we have things instead of the things having us.

Figurative darkness works the same way. If you spend your daylight hours with the pressures of work, studies, family obligations, being an informed world citizen, and chores and then seek to escape it all with movies, TV shows, video games, books, and (*yikes*) friends that are filled with darkness and despair, you're bound to feel sad and anxious.

Decide, instead, to fill your optional activities with programming and people that will bring you a laugh, a smile, or a sense of hope and connection.

Choose light whenever you can for an attitude that will make the hard times more tolerable and the fun times live up to their full potential.

THINGS TO KNOW BEFORE YOU GO

D IS FOR DETERMINATION

Time flies. Life is short. It seems like yesterday...

"Time can be an ally or an enemy. What it becomes depends entirely upon you, your goals, and your determination to use every available minute." — Zig Ziglar

There are so many ways to reflect on the passing of time and the emphasis on making the most of it. And while there's no doubt that when we all face the end of ours, we will feel that we could have and should have squeezed more out of the moments we were given.

That said, it's a pretty sure thing that all of those expressions were coined by people who were in the middle of a damn fine day. One that likely included some serious laughter and leisure. Those who are honest will admit that there are the opposite kinds of days, too, that feel like one eternal clustering of, shall we say, "ducks."

It is on these days that I find some unconventional inspiration in this thought: Life may, in fact, be too short, but it is somehow also *waaaaaaaay* too long to let it suck.

When too many days in a row feel like drudgery to me, with too many hours focused on thinking and accomplishing and not near enough focused on feeling and creating, it is high time to do some soul-searching, some pattern-breaking, and some ass-busting.

Of course, there will always be hours that must be devoted to work, studies, chores, and caring for friends and family members. We all have responsibilities that are no one's definition of fun and excitement, but this is life. But when there is zero time or energy left for anything that feeds your spirit, it's time to consider what can be cut to make way for something that brings a smile to your face, a twinkle to your eye, a sense of accomplishment that you are making progress toward the new version of YOU that you hunger for?

This is when determination needs to come in like a wrecking ball and linger like a winter chest cold.

As much as we would like our desires to spontaneously manifest themselves into our realities, our vision of what we want is really just the starting point.

Our daily question has to become: How hungry am I for a new normal? How am I going to lighten the load carried by my soul to take steps toward someplace better?

And it isn't just the tasks that need to be squeezed into our schedules. It's more than that. The real need for determination and conviction comes when we begin to defeat ourselves with negative thoughts.

The doubting demons whisper in our ear... *who do you think you are?* We start wondering if we are good enough to be accepted in this new role or version of ourselves that we hunger for.

The best way to slay this beast is to let him know that you don't expect to arrive "there" tomorrow—you simply need to take a step forward today. Because when you focus on the next step instead of the end goal, you are less daunted by the enormity of what you're trying to do, less overwhelmed by the zillions of tasks and mental shifts you will have to do and make, and less likely to buy in to the demon whispers.

It's no easy feat to slay those whispers, by the way. They creep in so easily because of the bombardment of media that enters our psyche each day as we scroll through one person's highlight reel after another, forgetting entirely that before the people we follow can share a picture of themselves winning a race, landing a role, getting a promotion or an engagement ring, taking a fancy trip, or losing a bunch of weight, they spend countless hours on the track, in the pool, rehearsing and training, working overtime, enduring heartbreak, staying in to save money, going hungry, and pushing through when it was so much easier to give up and sit down.

Every time we see their celebrations or hear about them in polite, social small talk, we must remind ourselves of the pain before the rising (as described by my hero, Glennon Doyle) so that we don't delude ourselves about the work we must put in before we can ever expect the victories and progress we crave.

There are no overnight successes and sensations. This is a myth we believe in because we want to think that we can wait around for a lottery-load of luck to attain the same. The reason these people have success is because of all the work and perseverance they put in long before you ever heard their name.

What work do you need to put in to move one step closer to what you want?

THINGS TO KNOW BEFORE YOU GO

E IS FOR EXERCISE YOUR WHOLE SELF

"Use it or lose it," as the trusty cliché goes... and it is as applicable to our brain as the body that houses it.

Whether our motivation to hit the gym, the bike trail, or the streets is to manage our stress or to manage our weight, the benefits are always twofold. Do it enough and we'll keep our pants *and* our arteries from getting tight.

Some of us pursue physical wellness with those coveted 10,000 steps, while others a perfectly formed pigeon pose, a six-minute mile, or a 200-pound deadlift. The key is that we just keep moving. In an era when many of us make a living sitting down, we need to get up and MOVE.

Move with enough frequency and you will feel less of the *ugh* stuff: less jiggly, less like going off on someone, and less withdrawn. Instead you will feel more of the *yessss* stuff: more vibrant, more in control, more confident, and more likely to participate in conversations.

Similarly, a mind that's consistently fed new knowledge creates new neural pathways that keep our brains fit medically, but also keep us feeling confident as vibrant, lifelong-learners.

We've all heard the expression, "knowledge is power." Well, pardon the pun, but isn't that a no-brainer? People who know things are considered intelligent. Those who are intelligent get better jobs than those who aren't. People who get good jobs are exposed to leadership opportunities that put them in a position of influence. Yes, knowledge is power.

The problem for many of us is that we have been conditioned to pursue the facade of intelligence over the true learning that sticks and becomes part of our mental bandwidth.

After spending a big part of our lives being evaluated on our performance at school, it's easy to forget that what matters more in life is the learning behind the GPA, rather than the numbers on the transcripts. We come by these grade-grubbing ways honestly, as the system makes us have to care about the numbers so we can qualify for the next level of our education or employment. The key, though, is in knowing early enough that focusing exclusively on the grade may leave us looking qualified for the next level of schooling, but not the next level of living.

In life, we don't get to walk around with our diploma hanging off a gold chain around our neck to announce our brilliance. We actually have to prove it in our daily interactions with people. Our competence becomes our calling card.

This means we need to focus less on performance and more on the acquiring of knowledge. We must let our curiosity guide the development of our mind so that it grows robustly by taking in the rich history of the people and places that surround us and by caring to understand how and why things work the way they do: whether it be our body, our mind, the electoral process, or the toaster oven.

Seek information. Seek stimulation. Seek a path that will grow you fat in the hat.

But there's another piece of us – a piece that often gets serviced last, if at all – that needs as much exercise as our body and brain, and that is our soul.

I'm guessing it's the most neglected part of us humans because it's the one piece of us that can't be seen or touched. Yet in all of its invisibility, it still manages to be the one part of you that is truly YOU.

So how can we exercise this part of ourselves, when it's often even hard to define?

I think the answer lies in this question: "What would you do if you knew you had one month to live?"

If your answer is centered in nature, then your soul's exercise is in seeking more sunsets and mountaintops, more oceans and rivers.

If your answer is centered in your beliefs in God, praise God. Find people who share your beliefs and worship with them.

If your answer is centered in music, stretch your soul's muscles by making regular time to create music, see live performances, get lost in your Spotify or iTunes account.

If your answer is centered in the people you love, then your soul's workout is to connect with these people. Whenever possible, do this in person so you can look deeply into their eyes, the only place where a soul can almost be seen. Take the time to have meaningful conversations with them, understand them, *love* them actively.

If you act as though the exercise of your body, your mind, **and** your soul is a non-negotiable, required part of every day (in whatever amount you can work into your day), you will know the true meaning of wellness.

THINGS TO KNOW BEFORE YOU GO

F is for... Friendship

F IS FOR FRIENDSHIP

When it comes to forming friendships, the folks at Facebook sum it up best.

Relationship status: It's complicated.

Why is friendship complicated? Because everyone will disappoint us at times.

People let us down because sometimes their needs don't line up with our own. When the people we love have the emotional and physical capacity to feel generous enough of spirit to put their own needs aside for us, it feels beautiful. When they don't? Not so much.

When we feel disappointed by the people we are not tied to forever by blood or by marriage vows, it can be tempting to cut ties.

Therein lies the "complicated."

But the truth is, we need people. Lots of them. We need a great, big cluster of folks who will both lift us from the floor of despair and raise us over their shoulders in triumph. We need them as much in the moments of triage as we do when busting out our own how-funky-is-your-chicken end-zone dance when we have a win we've fought hard to achieve.

So, who do we cut and who do we keep?

It sounds harsh when put that way, but if you are trying to live a positive life, you can't spend your days surrounded by negative people. To circle back to the thought that we are the average of the five people we spend the most time with, it is important that we spend our time with people who help create a micro culture of growth and peace and laughter to surround ourselves with.

How do you know if you have a keeper? By asking yourself how you feel after spending time with them.

If you feel like you can be exactly who you are without making excuses or pretending to agree with things you don't; if you can open up and reveal things that make your heart hurt or soar without feeling criticized; if you feel lighter in spirit; if you feel motivated to create, push forward on a goal, pursue further wellness, then, yes, you've got yourself a keeper.

It is messy getting to the point where a friendship crosses over the threshold of "is this person worth the hassle" to "this person is designated on the short list of 'my people' and qualifies for my unconditional love and acceptance."

Once you have done your unspoken Brownie bridging ceremony (once a Girl Scout, always a Girl Scout) with this person, it's time to double down on your investment and accept that friendship only works if you do.

Busy with the demands of work, your partner, and family? Yep, we all are. And yet our wellness depends on keeping the connections with our friends strong and mutually beneficial.

Will these friends sometimes piss you off? Like, a lot? YES. But you'll know you are a real, functional, wholehearted yet still imperfectly human grownup the minute you recognize that it goes both ways. For every quirky quality they possess that grates on your nerves, there is something equally annoying you do that they must tolerate in return. This is a fact.

And once you truly internalize it, you will find yourself far more accepting of your friends. This acceptance, by the way, automatically makes you a better friend. And guess what? When you *are* a better friend, you'll be surprised how much better your friends treat you.

Find friends worth making this commitment to and let them love you, as you love them, flaws and all.

is for...

Gratitude

G IS FOR GRATITUDE

It seems to be basic human nature to accomplish one goal and then set your sights on the next. Whether that goal is about your person or your acquiring of possessions, many of us have the tendency to turn into Veruca Salt from *Willy Wonka* and want the next thing, and want it now.

While it is noble and good to be on a continual course of self-betterment, it's equally important to be grateful for where we are right this minute.

We hear people say things like, "As soon as I graduate/finish this project/meet someone/get promoted/buy a house/have a family/retire, I'll be happy."

Poppycock.

After all, if you can't see *and savor* the things that are going well for you *right now*, why do you think you will instantly become satisfied with the next accomplishment or acquisition?

According to gratitude researchers Robert Emmons and Michael McCullough, grateful people are acutely aware of the good things that happen to them and don't take them for granted. Additionally, they make a point of expressing their appreciation for their good fortune in a sincere, heartfelt way. It's no real surprise, then, that grateful people are happier, healthier, and more energetic. They report fewer medical ailments and feelings of loneliness, stress, anxiety, and depression.

As a side note, these are the kinds of people that Willy Wonka *never* boots from The Chocolate Factory.

Forbes writer Erika Andersen says, "People who are grateful not only seek out more successes, they draw successes into their lives. When you are grateful, others like to be around you. Your appreciation includes and supports them. You help them see the positive elements inherent in daily life and to feel more hopeful about the possibility of future success."

Knowing that gratitude can make us happier and more successful, how do we cultivate more of it? Experts say to think of it as an emotional muscle that will grow and strengthen with intentional use. Just like squats that will build up your booty, exercising your appreciation for things going right in your life will sculpt you a tight sense of gratitude.

A simple way to start your practice is to place a vase and some scraps of paper on your kitchen counter. Then, at the end of every day, make yourself find one thing that went right, however small it may seem. Whether you write, "a great chat on the phone with my faraway BFF," or "The sun came out after three straight days of rain," or "my pants still fit," the point is to train your brain to look for the good around you.

Gratitude: it's the golden ticket!

THINGS TO KNOW BEFORE YOU GO

is for ...

Helpers

H IS FOR HELPERS

"When I was a boy and I would see scary things in the news, my mother would say to me, 'Look for the helpers. You will always find people who are helping.'" — Mr. (Fred) Rogers

"And when you do not find yourself in need of a helper, look around and see how you might be one." — Me, riding the coattails of the brilliant Fred Rogers

Helpers are all around you, quietly doing their good work. They are the courteous people who notice your full arms and hold open the door while offering a kind smile. They are your neighbors who bring up your garbage cans from the curb. They are the people who see a car accident and stop to provide assistance. They are the unassuming heroes who intervene when someone is being mistreated.

When you train your eyes to look for these do-gooders in your day-to-day comings and goings, you will notice them all over town, every day of the week.

And once you see them for the commonplace sight they are, it becomes so much easier to put the helper expectation on yourself.

Being a helper simply means that you make the choice to notice a difficult situation and make it a little bit better. Whether you're doing so through simple gestures of kindness that improve the vibe in the rooms you walk into by being friendly and inclusive to all who are present; going out of your way to help lighten someone's load; or stepping up in a crisis, prepared to perform an act of heroism when the need arises, you are helping. Each one of these decisions makes a difference to the people you assist, and to our collective sense of the humanity around us.

Most of us already enjoy the feel-good sensation that washes over us when we can tell we brought someone relief, but there's another side to embracing the helper mentality—and that is being able to graciously *receive* help.

When you allow someone to be there for you – whether it be a stranger in the doorway of Starbucks, a neighbor bringing a home-cooked meal when you're ill, or a friend who offers to wait with you for some scary test results – you're giving that person an opportunity to experience the warm fuzzies of being a helpful human, as well.

In many cases, you're also opening up an opportunity for a deeper sense of connection that can only be formed between two people who understand the value of mutual support. When you accept an offer of help, you are allowing someone to really see you and connect with you in a way that can generate a priceless sense of mutuality.

So, as Mr. Rogers taught us, do look for (and be grateful for) the helpers, but it's not a bad idea to start by looking for one in the mirror.

I IS FOR INTEGRITY

If integrity could sound just a little sexier, it could be considered a superpower. But then again, because it's within the reach of all of us mere mortals, it shouldn't sound so lofty that we think we'd need to rock a cape and tights before we strived for it.

Integrity means having strong moral principles that don't just roll off our tongues: they are integrated into the whole of who we are and should be on display in our every action.

Because integrity means being committed to diverting each of your instincts through a filter of your values before acting upon them, having a strong sense of integrity is really about slowing down and acting deliberately.

Before you can be deliberate, though, it's important to spend some time thinking about the person you want to be. If you don't name and declare (if only to yourself) what you stand for, you are destined to make on-the-fly decisions that leave you with regret. And if you do this too many times, it may well jeopardize your feelings of self-worth.

So, ask yourself how committed you are to values like loyalty, respect, honesty, reliability, integrity, curiosity, and persistence. You will be much more likely to act spontaneously in accordance with such values if you've taken the time to really reflect on what you believe and who you want to be.

Then, let your superpower be The Pause by asking yourself: *Does what I'm about to do line up with what I claim to care about?*

Do you claim to value being an upstander? If so, are you speaking up when you see someone being treated unfairly?

Do you respect other people's time? If so, do you show up on time for meetings? Do you call them back when you say you will? Do you keep the social plans you make with them, or cancel when you get a better offer?

Are you the same person when people are watching as when you think they are not?

As much as I would like us humans to choose integrity because it is the morally right choice, the truth is that, in modern society, it's also the practical one. Technology pretty much assures that any indiscretion a person would be tempted to explore is going to come to light (or video). We have to assume that everything we do or say is being recorded in some way that can do one of two things: incriminate our shadiness or validate our virtue... it all depends on how we choose to act.

Why not know the ultimate sense of peace by actively deciding every day to live with a clear conscience.

People who do this consistently – as in way more often than not– have the strongest kind of personal "credit" rating. They are a safe, secure investment to the people who interact with them because of their consistent track record of knowing what is right and acting on that belief.

The doors that open for them in the form of referrals and recommendations for work, and the strong, trusting personal relationships they enjoy because of this are priceless.

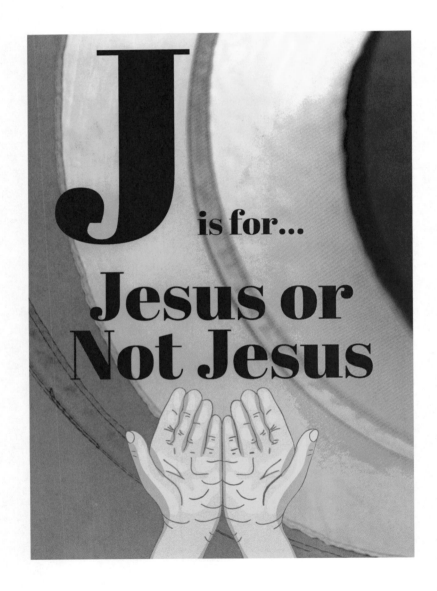

J is for...
Jesus or Not Jesus

J IS FOR JESUS OR NOT JESUS

It's no secret that religion is one of those topics that can tear people apart from one another just as easily as it can bring them together.

While many people have strong opinions as to whether you should believe in their version of God or in no God at all, there are just as many who are satisfied that you would believe in some force greater than yourself that inspires you to bring out your best possible YOU.

Whatever your faith or spirituality, I hope it leads you to express gratitude for the blessings in your life.

Whether the blessings you give thanks for are for shelter from the day's forecasted high of 100 (or low of 32), the luxury of a satisfied appetite, or that the people whom you care about are all healthy enough to give life a bunch more inhales and exhales as they celebrate their daily moments of joy and victory, or rise determined against a hairy challenge, I hope that gratitude washes over you each day in a moment of quiet reflection for all the things going right in your life.

On those days when it feels like there's little to be grateful for, I hope your faith brings you hope for a better tomorrow.

If you feel scared or alone, may it help you see that what currently feels desperate and unfathomable may be endured with one prayer or positive thought followed by another until the pain has lessened enough that you can move forward.

My wish is that these inner expressions of gratitude and hope give way to outward interactions that demonstrate your connection to a higher purpose as you treat others – both those who share your faith and those who don't – with respect, tolerance, patience, generosity, and sincerity. It is the only way you – and we – will know peace.

May you always believe in that someone or something that makes you want to do better and be better... for yourself and for the impact you can have on the world around you.

"Faith is the strength by which a shattered world will emerge into the light." — Helen Keller

THINGS TO KNOW BEFORE YOU GO

K IS FOR KINDNESS

"Be kind, for everyone you meet is fighting a hard battle."
— Ian Maclaren

In the whipping and whirling pace of modern living, many people feel invisible; when they aren't being met with aggression and disdain.

It's hard not to take the meanness personally, but the truth is that people who behave online or in person with snark and who snipe and snub and bully their way through your life are hiding a very important message inside their cruelty: It has nothing to do with you and everything to do with how they feel about themselves and the state of their own lives.

Their subconscious modus operandi reads: "I feel really crappy about who I am, but since I have no idea how to make myself feel better, I will just knock the people around me down a few notches so that we all feel similarly miserable. After all, it's easier to ruin your day (or life) than fix mine."

Or to put it in the words of mental health professionals: "Hurt people hurt people."

The problem is that there is no scarcity of hurt people, which makes me wonder what it would be like if we could read the minds of the strangers we pass on the streets. My guess is that, on any crowded street of pedestrians, there are people passing by with each of these concerns...

How will I pay these bills? Will the medicine work? Will he make it until I can get there? How am I going to get that done in time? Why didn't I get that job? How will I get there? Will I ever get to sleep? What will we eat? Is that a lump? Does anyone care?

Does knowing this excuse the behavior of the hurt people who seem hell bent on hurting people? Nope. But it does allow us to channel some of the pain we feel when exposed to their wrath into a sense of pity (or, ideally, compassion) for them.

As horrible as it is to experience these kinds of people, I have discovered that they add the kind of texture and context to our collective experience as humans that propels us to take action.

In the same way that having a brutal migraine brings me a euphoric sense of gratitude for the day after it clears, which would just be an ordinary day if not for the juxtaposition to the hellish day before, I believe we can't really appreciate the importance of kindness without being exposed to its true opposite.

Experiencing ugliness up close is what gives us the conviction to spread kindness to balance out the damage done by those hurt people who are determined to continue hurting people. They inspire us to choose, instead, to operate with an eye out for the needs of others, with a generous and inclusive spirit that creates kinship, community, and a sense of belonging for the people who need it (i.e. all of us).

SHANA MCLEAN MOORE

60SHANA MCLEAN MOORE

L IS FOR LOYALTY

Not to get all Mafioso on you, but loyalty is everything.

In fact, it is the primary expectation most of us have for anyone we consider family, friend, or partner. And by virtue of being an *expectation* – an almost *duh gee*, of course I presume you will be loyal to me if I consider you one of my people – it's a quality we tend to take for granted.

We sure shouldn't.

After all, the ability to know right down to our core that the people we care about are loyal to us is about as good of a feeling there is. It carries with it the type of security that makes us feel strong, valued, and capable of taking risks to grow and learn new things.

Having loyal people around us becomes our emotional safety net, allowing us to walk the ten-story tight ropes of our lives, without feeling like it will all end in *splat*.

Unfortunately, the reverse is also true. When there's evidence (even if only in our gut) that we've been betrayed by someone whom we presumed to be loyal, that net is pulled out from under us during a free fall. It comes as such a shock that it really feels like it *has* all ended in splat.

Here's the tricky part: we all want and expect loyalty from others, but often forget that some of the choices we make undermine our loved ones' ability to trust *us*.

Since it's often harder to see our own flaws than it is to see those of others, here's a quick test to see if you treat the people you care about with loyalty:

1. How would you feel about a breach in security that meant there was no way to password-protect your phone? If your boyfriend, girlfriend, or spouse could read your messages, how much explaining would you have to do? How much would you panic? Your reaction, whether it's "Oh $%#*, I'm busted!" or "No big deal," will tell you everything you need to know about the loyalty you offer.

2. When you repeat something you have heard about a friend or acquaintance, how do you feel the next time you run into the person whose back you talked behind? If you feel nervous or guilty, you have your answer about the loyalty you provide this person.

Loyalty is all about the reciprocity of trust: you simply cannot expect it if you can't provide it in return. And given all the benefits we receive from the people who are loyal to us, we would be fools not to give it out with great gusto.

A relationship of any kind that offers you less than reciprocated loyalty? Fuhgeddaboudit!

THINGS TO KNOW BEFORE YOU GO

M IS FOR MODERATION

Wait. Wait. Wait. Before you turn the page to avoid the least sexy topic of all time, please hear me out.

Think about the last few times you have been involved with drama.

Mhmmm.

How much were people drinking, smoking, or otherwise impairing their judgment?

When we humans want to let go and let loose, we don't have the precision to selectively pickle the part of our brain that allows us to feel fun and free and less self-conscious without also shutting down the part that says, "let's still be thoughtful and respectful of others so that we're all still friends when this stuff wears off."

Just when we start feeling "*woo-hoo*" we seem to forget that the truth can hurt, especially once our filter has become anesthetized and we're hell bent on telling it how it *really* is.

Then there's the whole primal urge thing that leaves some people determined to prove their sexiness by flirting (or worse) with other people's partners.

The other aspect of partying that is dangerous is not being able to see in yourself that what started out as occasional social fun is transitioning, slowly but surely, into a dependency that can ruin relationships and careers and your physical health.

We all know someone who self-destructed in this way, don't we?

What likely started as a beer or social smoke with friends escalated to a daily high that started making homework/work/engaging with their loved ones feel optional, and eventually made attending class/meetings/family dinners feel like a waste of time. And then, well, there were bigger and better highs to get, so what started out as "just weed" became "just pills."

Then, in what felt like all of a sudden, but was really a bunch of baby steps that lined up to nowhere... they were "just" out of plans for the future, "just" out of having the motivation to make any, and "just" out of people who wanted to put up with their shit.

You probably know other people who seem to smoke a little weed, get drunk on weekends, and manage their work life and relationships without any apparent ill effects. It's true— some people can do that. But the scary news is that you often don't find out that *you* can't until it's too late.

For some people, even social partying wreaks havoc with their brain chemistry. They go all in and can't seem to come back. Or they are given drugs that aren't as harmless as they were billed to be. And the people you once knew are gone.

I recognize (and appreciate) social drinking as part of our culture, but take it from me: one cocktail per hour is plenty. Any more and you will likely say and do things you regret, whether it be with the wrong company or the wrong interactions with the right company.

Try moderation and watch how the drama in your life decreases.

If you are comfortable in your own skin, you don't need to put on a drug disguise to be able to connect with other people and have fun.

The brutal truth is, the difficult emotions you are trying to escape for the night will still be there in the morning (perhaps with some new ones), so it is best to feel what needs to be felt and pursue constructive ways to cope with them.

N IS FOR NEXT...

Dear actor/singer/filmmaker/athlete/writer/med-business-law school applicant,

We regret to inform you that we cannot accept you to our roster/program at this time. Thank you for considering us and we wish you the best in your pursuits.

Sincerely,

The Dream Crushers

We've all been disappointed in a "No." Whether it is a personal relationship or an academic or career pursuit, our dreams can be bigger than our current abilities.

But does this mean we shouldn't have any dreams for ourselves in order to avoid disappointment?

Hell no.

"Grit is that 'extra something' that separates the most successful people from the rest. It's the passion, perseverance, and stamina that we must channel in order to stick with our dreams until they become a reality." — Travis Bradberry

In fact, no matter your passion, there are success stories that can look like overnight fairytales until you delve into the backstories. The people who have reached the apex of success in their fields, who make a career out of doing something they love and also make a gazillion dollars in the process, also faced setbacks.

Twelve publishers passed on J.K. Rowling's *Harry Potter and the Philosopher's Stone* before the series went on to make more than $450 million, taking the author from welfare to the *Forbes* list of the world's most wealthy.

Walt Disney was fired from the *Kansas City Star* because he "lacked imagination and had no good ideas."

Michael Jordan was cut from his high school basketball team.

Oprah Winfrey was fired from a news station because her emotions got in the way.

Steven Spielberg was rejected from the University of Southern California School of Theater, Film, and Television three times before dropping out of college altogether and becoming one of the most iconic directors in Hollywood.

Actress Chrissy Metz had 81 cents in her bank account when she landed the role of her lifetime in *This is Us*.

Sure, you can say that it's statistically improbable that those of us who have the same dreams and ambitions will ever reach their level of success. Fair enough.

But the thing is, we take those odds from slim to zero if we give up before we really try. And even if we can't get to that level of success, there are still many emotional benefits to doing something we really enjoy.

Whether it is an academic, athletic, artistic, or simply a modest goal of personal betterment, the message is the same:

You will, at times, come up short, outright fail and feel defeated. You will feel like only a masochist would keep the path you're on and tolerate so little reward. But what will set you apart and get you closer and closer to the goal you hunger to achieve is your commitment to your next step forward.

Do not be deterred by rejection. Keep learning and growing so that you continue to improve. And while others may quit the course out of discouragement, you will continue your ascent as you not only preserve, but get better and better as you go.

Make this your internal reply to any naysayers who come your way:

"Dear acceptance board/casting director/literary agent/coach/prospective employer, I see you choose to watch me rise from afar. Okay, next..."

O IS FOR OWN IT

As my guru Oprah would say: you really need to OWN it—your good, your bad, *and* your ugly.

While most of us can identify what it is we do well, we need to remember that it's just as important to pinpoint where we fall short. Owning our mistakes and shortcomings is an essential part of living harmoniously with others and ourselves.

Once we see our faults, declare them, and own them with our words, we can start working on a plan to change what can be changed, come to peace with what cannot, and make any appropriate apologies so that people will want to continue to be our friends and loved ones.

This kind of self-awareness allows us to write the curriculum for our own Master Class.

Are you often late to meetings, both for work and pleasure? Notice this about yourself. Acknowledge that you are being disrespectful of other people's time, which is just as valuable as whatever you deemed more important than being punctual for this person. If you do this once or twice, an apology is probably enough. If it happens more often than that, know that your time management problems make you rude. Start being realistic about how much time each of your obligations takes and plan your day accordingly.

Do you have trouble apologizing when you've hurt someone's feelings or said things in anger? We all get ugly when hormones, exhaustion, or hunger act like accelerants to our internal blaze. The first step is to go back to the person who was on the receiving end of your burn and apologize. Again, the apology only works when needed sparingly. If you have these kinds of blowups with regularity, it's time to dig deeper and work on real changes: seek medication for the hormones, solid sleep for the exhaustion, and healthy eating to ward off another "hangry" moment.

How often do you avoid pulling your weight in any team dynamic? Whether it is as a partner, colleague, friend, or family member, are you making these relationships mutually beneficial, or are you the group taker? Don't wait for others to point out your selfish tendencies—confront them head on by saying, "It's my turn to step up, let me take that on." And then honor your commitment.

Once we can list and own our shortcomings, we can work on wiping out the shame, blame, and denial that accompany them. And by owning all of who we are as our work-in-progress selves, we're headed toward the making of our own best life.

THINGS TO KNOW BEFORE YOU GO

P IS FOR (BE) PRESENT

In this age of constant texting and social media monitoring, the act of giving someone your real-time, face-to-face presence and focus is the ultimate connection.

As an added bonus, it doesn't even require a password— only your undivided attention.

In these times of perpetual multi-tasking, being engaged eye-to-eye and truly hearing and responding to the thoughts and ideas of another human being leaves a noteworthy impression on the people you spend time with. People walk away from their time spent with you feeling listened to, understood, valued, cared about, and validated.

When you have these kinds of interactions with people, what do you want to do? You want to schedule the next one. Why? Because you feel good.

Sadly, the reverse is also true. We've all spent time with someone who either ignored us for an awkwardly long period of time, or pretended to be paying attention with the token

"Mhm… *really*?" while they typed away on their phone. This is no big deal if it happens for a moment and then the person apologizes and puts their phone down. But if it happens repeatedly, what message are they really giving you? You – the person who took time out of their own busy day to sit down and share a meal or a moment with them – are not as important as the person (or followers) they're typing to.

How do you feel walking away from that kind of interaction? Like someone who just wasted their time on a person who's just not that into you.

Do you want to book the next one of those meet-ups? Hell no.

When you gather with people, put your phone away and prove to them that they matter by being truly present in your interaction with them. Be someone people want to connect with time and again by making them feel valued. The good vibes will come right back to you as you attract people who value connection like you do.

THINGS TO KNOW BEFORE YOU GO

Q IS FOR QUIET

Shhhhhh. Stop talking. Shut up. Quell your impulse to interject, to disturb the silence. Be quiet.

Does that sound weird coming from a gal who always has something to say and encourages you to do the same? I hope not because even though it's important to be an active participant in thoughtful and engaging conversations, it's equally important to focus on being the kind of person who hears, who listens, who understands.

For one thing, when you're quiet, you learn things, whether it be facts and figures that can really sink into your consciousness when uninterrupted by chatter, or the nuances of what a loved one is saying in the pauses between their spoken words.

You aren't learning anything when you're talking.

– Lyndon B. Johnson

Allowing others time to talk and then truly listening to them, even when you're dying to tell a story of your own, also makes you more likeable. Everyone *wants* to be heard, just like you do. But most people don't feel understood. If you can be known as the person who cares enough to listen and reflect back the messages you receive, you will become beloved.

People who don't understand the importance of real dialogue hold court for what feels like forever to their captive audience, coming off as arrogant and selfish. Instead, invite people in by pausing and allowing them to agree or disagree with you, instead of making them feel like they are in a 500-seat lecture hall.

Knowing when to be quiet also allows you to avoid looking like an ass. We've all been around the annoying person who spouts off like they're the expert about something they know little or nothing about. *Blech*. No one wants to be around that person. If you truly don't have an informed opinion about something, it's the perfect time to button your trap, zip your lip, shut your pie hole... be quiet.

THINGS TO KNOW BEFORE YOU GO

R,
is for...
Reflect

R IS FOR REFLECT

Reflection is a beautiful thing; usually brought on by big birthdays, graduations, breakups, or a lonely Saturday night thumbing through your photo stream.

It's when you take the time to ponder how you got where you are and take inventory of who is still sitting beside you.

Sometimes the act of reflecting brings a wave of gratitude for the way things are working out, while other times it makes you melancholy for the way things used to be.

Whether you're currently feeling "pinch-me-how-can-I-be-so-lucky" or seven depths of sad, it's always a good idea to stop and ponder what led you to where you are.

If things feel good for you right now, with plenty of people to help you celebrate your birthday, if your graduation feels more like a celebration of what's to come than what's over, or if you're moving on from a toxic relationship, know that none of this happened by accident.

It means you worked hard to treat people well. Your family and friends are there for you because you were there for them during their times of joy and sorrow. You treated them with compassion, loyalty, and a we-are-a-team attitude. Let your reflection on the beauty and necessity of mutually supportive and loving relationships make you recommit yourself to keep this going, because it brings you so much in return.

If you're celebrating a graduation or promotion, with exciting plans ahead, it means you missed out on some fun while working your tail off for those good grades. Reflect on the discipline it took. Promise yourself that you will dig just as deep for the challenges that lie ahead so that you may feel this deep sense of accomplishment and hope and excitement for the future, once again.

If you're celebrating the end of a toxic relationship that stifled you, reflect on how it went wrong so you won't make the same mistakes again. Appreciate and grow your feelings of self-worth by focusing on the lessons instead of the pain. How are you different now than when you accepted being mistreated?

When things aren't going well, reflection is just as important. When you're really hurting, it will be tempting to blame other people for your plight, but that only takes you half way out of trouble. You need to also reflect on what YOU did or didn't do to nurture your relationships, succeed in your school or work, or accept being mistreated by others.

If you're lonely, did people leave you out because they are cruel, or could you have been more inclusive, a better listener, less of a downer? Take an honest walk through your memory and decide where things went wrong.

If you're struggling at work or with your classes, is your boss or teacher really to blame? Or are you taking shortcuts and getting sloppy with the quality of your work? The only way to really know is to reflect on your actions. Honestly. Regularly.

With enough time spent reflecting, more of what you're evaluating will make you feel proud of how you handled both situations and people.

S
is for...
Sexiness

S IS FOR SEXINESS

Save for the one-hit-wonder band LMFAO, people don't really walk around declaring, "I'm sexy and I know it." I mean, heck, even Beyoncé doesn't claim it outright.

In fact, the second you declare sexy as your very own adjective, you've pretty much fallen to "not even" on anyone's hot-or-not list. Why, you ask? Because people with sex appeal don't need to talk about it; they know it isn't even a trait one can set out to have. Instead, sexiness is the cumulative impression of your whole self, which is composed as much by your spirit as it is by the vessel it struts in.

Do people see you as confident, fun, motivated, intelligent, kind (but not a pushover), interesting, and independent? Yes? Then, by golly, you're sexy.

Why? Because these qualities make you walk into a room like you belong there. You look people in the eye and have something to talk about. Your sexiness is in your every word and every step. It's in the way you listen and laugh and engage.

People who don't understand this are looking for a quick-fix way to grab attention. And it usually involves a blatant display of T & A (this means Tits and Ass, youngins). This display is most evident in the little tight dress that just barely covers your booty so that every two steps in your five-inch heels requires you to tug it down so your butt doesn't actually pop out the bottom. This dress also scoops low in the chest and maybe even includes a cutout or two. And if it could talk, it would be yelling, "Hey, guys! Look what I have here! Aren't I sexy?!"

Nope. You're actually trying too hard, and sexy people don't have to do that.

Whatever you decide to put on, *wear it*— don't let it wear you. Let your sexiness exude subtly from your spirit so you don't have to go proving that you have "passion in your pants and you ain't afraid to show it."

That's sexy... and you know it.

THINGS TO KNOW BEFORE YOU GO

T IS FOR TENDERNESS

Cradling a newborn baby. Rubbing the belly of a sleeping puppy. The gentle way we embrace a beloved granny.

Tenderness feels so soft and mushy that it would be easy to think of it as a weakness. After all, tenderness is most visible in a cuddle, hardly the stuff of tough guys. But even though it goes against our logical mind to see snuggling as the stuff of badasses, it actually is.

Why? Because every time one person extends their arms to another, they risk feeling rejected.

Making yourself vulnerable by reaching out, despite the risk of being rebuffed, qualifies you as strong. Not in the "I-can-kick-your-ass" sense, but in the "I-will-expose-the-most-fragile-piece-of-my-heart-to-you-at-the-risk-of-you-breaking-it-to-smithereens" sense.

People with this type of strength won't be able to show it off in the form of a six-pack of abdominal muscles, but inside they have a spirit that is as ripped as any gym rat's biceps.

It's a risk I hope you'll take.

Whether you express tenderness through the words you choose to show concern or empathy to someone who is struggling, or by connecting with someone physically, we know you will feel the benefits as much as the person who receives your warmth.

People need tenderness. YOU need it.

Life can be hard and lonely at times. Human tenderness is the antidote to the pain we feel. When someone extends a hand when we're crying or hears us out as we pour out our hearts, we begin to feel the sense of hope and connection that we're aching for.

Human touch is powerful and the sad fact is that most people give it and receive it less as they age. According to studies by the University of Miami's Touch Research Institute, human touch has a wide range of physical and emotional benefits for people of all ages. Touch lessens pain, improves lung functioning, increases growth in infants, lowers blood glucose levels, and improves immune system functioning.

Yet with all the benefits of touch, these studies indicate that by the time a child becomes a teenager, they receive half as much touching as they did as small children. This continues to decline with age, with senior citizens receiving the smallest amounts of touch of all groups.

I hope you will remember this the next time you greet someone you care about. Instead of just sharing a hello, why not open your arms to greet them with a hug?

Your friendly touch will increase the release of oxytocin, the "cuddle hormone" that helps promote feelings of devotion, trust, and bonding. In **both** of you.

Show your emotional mettle and reach out today to offer some tenderness.

U is for...
Uniquely
YOU

U IS FOR UNIQUELY YOU

"I think the reward for conformity is that everyone likes you except yourself." — Rita Mae Brown

We humans are pack animals and we long to belong.

The problem is that many of us, especially during our school years, will go to great lengths to convince ourselves that we like certain music, lifestyles, and bitchy popular people that we actually can't stand in order to avoid feeling like outcasts. And if we still can't belong, we think let us at least blend in enough so that no one targets us as the pariahs we feel like.

Am I right?

All of this isn't too damaging to the people who are happy to conform or, perhaps, to those who have the social clout to determine what the others should conform to, but for the others? It is misery.

Until they break free.

Often this doesn't happen until a person can move away to a new town and meet people they connect with naturally instead of being forced together based upon their parents' zip code.

Eventually it happens, though— it sinks in for all of us that the people who make our eyes light up most when we see them coming our way are the ones who stand out in the crowd instead of blending into it.

So, what it is about them? Are they notably funny? Quirky? Creative? Smart as a whip? Compassionate? Empathetic? Driven?

Whatever the reason, our conversations with these people who sit authentically in their uniqueness are stimulating because they open our minds to different ways of thinking. Our social life opens up and feels exciting when we spend time with them because they introduce us to people and events we wouldn't have discovered without them.

Whenever you meet someone who has this effect on you, use it as your evidence that conformity is overrated so that you are more likely to embrace the ways in which YOU are unique. Do not hide the ways in which you are different in order to fit in. Instead, seek the company of people who value such individuality so you can give one another the validation you deserve.

You will feel more free and alive than ever before when you are uniquely YOU.

THINGS TO KNOW BEFORE YOU GO

V IS FOR VULNERABILITY

Target. Victim. Weak. Prey.

The first association many people have with vulnerability reflects its definition, "the quality or state of being exposed to the possibility of being attacked or harmed, either physically or emotionally."

An image search of the word of "vulnerable" shows newborn kittens, innocent infants, and broken people cowering in corners.

After an eyeful of that, nobody's signing up for the vulnerability club.

But there's another side to vulnerability. It's a side explored by research professor Brené Brown. If you're one of the 32 million people who've watched her TED Talk on the subject, you might already agree with her conclusion that vulnerability is actually the ultimate form of bravery.

How can a change in perspective take a cowering kitty to king of the jungle? Because vulnerability requires us to show up and be seen exactly as who we are. (*Gulp.* Even the parts we're not proud of.)

In addition to having to own all of who we are, Brown says that vulnerability also requires us to "wake up every day and love someone who may or may not love us back, whose safety we can't ensure, who may stay in our lives or may leave without a moment's notice, who may be loyal to the day they die or betray us tomorrow."

Scary, right?

By being our true and imperfect selves and committing ourselves to love without guarantees, we *are* exposed. And we are, indeed, "susceptible to being wounded or hurt."

But here's the thing, what we're getting in return for all that risk is something far richer than what we could ever experience when living guarded and untrusting.

It's something of the old "I'll show you mine if you show me yours" routine, which implies that both parties might feel they are inadequate but muster up the courage to find out together.

It's being able to whisper to someone...

I love you... do you love me?

I'm scared to visit the doctor.

I'm not sure how I will ever pay off these student loans.

In my 50 years on earth, I have talked to enough people to know that every single person on this planet has doubts and fears of not measuring up. I have them too. And it's easy to get into the habit of focusing on yours and feeling alone and inadequate in them.

Until, that is, we have a real and vulnerable conversation with someone who resets our perspective.

I got my reminder yesterday when listening to my friend's daughter who's feeling defeated by the college acceptance process. She's feeling fearful that her number-one choice won't want her.

Sitting across from her, I saw a young woman who shouldn't have anything but excitement for what lies ahead. She's smart, funny, feisty, kind, centered, and vivacious. She has the world at her fingertips, from my vantage point, whether she gets into her first-choice school or her fifth.

For her, though, it's a make-or-break moment that's leaving her feeling exposed, anxious, and unworthy.

As she shared this vulnerability with me, she opened me up to sharing mine with her. I know we both left that meeting feeling a little lighter and more connected. We were both reminded that every one of us has tender spots not visible to casual onlookers.

In opening up to each other, we're helping redefine vulnerability in the Brené Brown way... by becoming "susceptible to having deep and meaningful relationships; open to love and connection."

W

is for...

Worthiness

VIP

W IS FOR WORTHINESS

"We're not worthy!" — Wayne and Garth, Wayne's World

"Yes you are!" — Me

When you fall in love while operating under the idea that you *deserve* this love, you don't have to waste your time, energy, and sleuthing skills worrying about how and when this person might betray you.

This is because you know you're enough, right here and right now.

Does this mean you don't have aspects of yourself that could be improved? Of course not. It just means that you understand that this person chose to be your friend, your lover, and your confidant as the imperfectly lovable person you already are.

If you can make peace with yourself in this way, you will never become the nightmarish stage-five clinger girlfriend or boyfriend who feels threatened by every call, text, or visit that comes your partner's way. You won't need to know their passwords, check their history, sneak through drawers and pockets, stalk their Instagram followers, or go all CSI on them.

Instead of stalking, you must be able to say to yourself in your most sincere voice: "Why would he/she want to be with someone else?"

If you can't say that and *believe* it, then it just might be time to party on elsewhere, Garth.

The next question is simple: Is it you or is it them? If your partner is attentive, available, and not acting shady, the problem lies in your feelings of self-worth. If reminding yourself that there's a reason they chose you isn't enough, then it could be time to explore counseling. Because you will never have a healthy relationship until you believe you deserve one.

If the problem is that your partner is behaving in a way that doesn't make you feel special or secure – by being unavailable, unsupportive, or uninterested – and shows no desire to change, then it's time to recognize this union as a mismatch and move on. Because, by virtue of being alive, you are worthy of love.

THINGS TO KNOW BEFORE YOU GO

X IS FOR EXPLORE

"The World is a book, and those who do not travel read only a page." — Saint Augustine

We don't often notice the utter routineness of our lives until we snap out of it by being called away for a graduation, wedding, business trip, family emergency, or spontaneous escape.

Getting away, near or far, awakens our senses. By breaking out of our routine and away from our home base, we are confronted with new sights to see, new flavors to taste, new scents to smell, and different voices and sounds to hear. We're drawn out of autopilot mode and are forced to pay more attention to everything around us.

The result is that we suddenly feel more alive.

Whether your budget and calendar afford you a weekend stay at a friend's house out of town or an adventurous trip to faraway lands, I urge you to go.

Explore.

Get a change of scenery, a fresh perspective.

I hope you'll open your mind the best way one can: by seeing people live differently than you do, yet be content anyway. It will enable you to learn firsthand that there are many ways to live a satisfying life. It may even challenge you to examine your own approach, leaving you feeling either validated in the choices you've made, or motivated to consider new ones.

Indeed, travel will teach you tolerance of people's differences, but it will also teach you the fundamental sameness of the human condition. Maya Angelou said it best when she said, "Perhaps travel cannot prevent bigotry, but by demonstrating that all peoples cry, laugh, eat, worry, and die, it can introduce the idea that if we try and understand each other, we may even become friends."

The farther you travel, the more of these revelations await you:

You will find yourself lost, very lost, and have to navigate new towns, many times even in new languages.

You will find yourself hungry and feeling rude to refuse local delicacies that you'd never try at home.

You will see new kinds of beauty in nature, architecture, and in the faces of people who look nothing like you.

You will gain a new understanding of history by seeing structures and artifacts that redefine your designation of "old" and "new."

You will discover an appreciation for the blasé way with which you use your country's currency, your native tongue, your nation's bureaucracy.

You will find yourself aching with loneliness for people and for the comforts and ease of being home—making you really understand who you miss and how much they mean to you, and how fortunate you are for each of the comforts of home that you previously took for granted.

You will discover strengths you never knew you had by navigating all of this unfamiliarity.

With each page you turn in the World book Saint Augustine referred to, you will grow and discover and appreciate.

Read every page you can get your hands on.

SHANA MCLEAN MOORE

Y IS FOR YEARN

"Where does discontent start? You are warm enough, but you shiver. You are fed, yet hunger gnaws you. You have been loved, but your yearning wanders in new fields. And to prod all these there's time, the Bastard Time."

— John Steinbeck

Let's face it, at first glance, yearning seems like nothing more than the fancy man's word for wanting. To put it visually, Want comes in wearing jeans and a T-shirt, while Yearn bursts through the door with a long stride, wearing a suit, tie, and a furrowed brow.

Yearning, you see, is serious business.

What do *you* want that badly? What do you covet, crave, itch, pine, thirst, and long for?

People who have this hunger often accomplish big things, so don't ever apologize for it. But make sure those feelings are directed at a really specific target. Ideally this focus will be at the bull's-eye center of a clearly defined ring of smaller goals that lead incrementally (and achievably) to the piercing center.

The alternative can be bleak for those who don't take the time to articulate what it is that they are aching to accomplish and wind up seeing their unfocused angst turn into misery.

To modernize Steinbeck's thoughts on this subject, "Ain't nobody got time for that."

This means that it's essential to spend time really defining what it is you want, because only then can you develop a plan of action.

With plan in hand, you become the kind of person who is exciting to be around because all the passion behind your longing becomes a contagious can-do spirit.

While chasing your goals, though, it is important that these desires that make you want to push, to strive, to pursue with great passion also be accompanied by a spirit of gratitude for all that is already right with your life.

So, direct the fire inside you at your future, but don't forget to bask in both the glow of the accomplishments you've already made and the intangible things like having people to love and good health that make everything else possible.

Let that yearning of yours wander a bit into new fields, but then give it some direction – and perspective – so there's no need to fear Bastard Time.

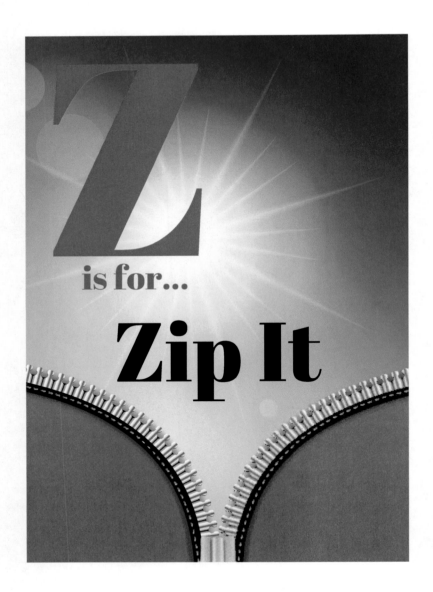

Z IS FOR ZIP IT

Sex can happen between any two people bold enough to get naked together, but the kind of sex that inhabits (or haunts) our hearts requires that we have emotional intimacy with our partner before we even consider seeking the physical kind.

I will leave out the sordid details that prove my credentials on the subject (you're welcome, kids), but be assured that I speak from experience of the non-Puritan variety when I say it to be true.

So what does emotional intimacy really mean?

It means that you've gotten a glimpse into this person's soul and you've deemed it worthy of your trust.

It means that you know this person well enough that when the act is over, you won't feel weird or, worse yet, used.

It means that you don't have to wonder if this person will text, call, or see you again, because they are already invested in you as a human being—not just a receptacle for their lust.

Not everyone will agree, but to me, this means that one-night stands offer you nothing. Why would you share your biology and a piece of your soul with someone who doesn't really know you? Sure, they may wake up and be able to recite your name, rank, and serial number, but do they have any clue about your goals and dreams, your fears and worries? The qualities that make you uniquely you?

So, I say this to you straight: a union that starts with a climax (that probably won't be yours) instead of building to one, has no place to go but toward an awkward end.

"Good morning. I realize you've made the acquaintance of my privates after some prosecco, so would you be interested in getting to know my communication style over a cup of coffee?"

What? Too awkward?

Friend, you simply can't turn a wild night into a healthy relationship. Instead, you'll wake up awash in emotional emptiness, and perhaps even a mindful of worry over the possibility of unwanted pregnancy or an STD.

With much love and motherly wisdom, I ask you to keep your pants zipped and either offer up or wait for an invitation for a real first date. And then somewhere between 9 and 99 more.

Sorry if felt like that was delivered by a woman in a bonnet and petticoat, but I hope you get the idea… if you haven't let them into your heart, please don't let them into your body.

CONCLUSION

My wish for you, dear daughter/son/friend/stranger/myself in need of a reminder, is that you will continue down your path of adulthood with a whole heart—one that is open to adventure, love, and success in whatever way you define it for yourself.

Be kind to yourself whenever you fall, for it is these very mistakes that will grow and stretch you. They will give you the thick skin you will need when times get hard, as they do for every single one of us, young and old.

On those days when you feel like a failure, confide in someone you trust—a friend/mentor/your mama who will hear you out without too much judgment or unsolicited advice. (Well, the unsolicited advice thing is hard for mamas.)

Sharing these vulnerable feelings releases so much of the pressure that's crippling you from getting up and moving on past the hardships.

When you share your tender spots with people, you will be reminded that we all have them. Just because people walk around with a smile or a stern expression of emotional armor around them, it doesn't mean that they aren't hurting just as much inside. Or more.

Knowing that we all walk around with memories of pain or fresh hurt, disappointments, and frustrations – no matter how put together we look to outsiders — is somehow comforting. It makes us feel like we aren't alone in our struggles and imperfections.

It also allows us to forgive the people around us: the strangers who cut us off on the road, the inconsiderate neighbor who parks too close to our car, the friend who forgets our birthday, and the loved one who doesn't seem able to give us what we want at any given moment.

Keeping this in mind reminds us to always be kind, to ourselves and others.

Whether you are reading this as someone's beloved child, beloved parent or both, I hope that these A-to-Z lessons ring in your ear as you go about the many new experiences that lie ahead of you.

My wish for you is that you always: keep the company of the AWESOME people around you who inspire you to raise your game; be BRAVE by risking rejection to pursue the new opportunities you yearn for or by standing up for yourself or others who need an ally; and CHOOSE a good attitude when a bad one would be so much easier.

May these grownup ABCs serve you well on your journey to wholehearted and wholly awesome living.

With love,

Shana/Mom/Myself in need of the reminder

THINGS TO KNOW BEFORE YOU GO

39010284R00073

Made in the USA
Middletown, DE
13 March 2019